engage

Starter

Workbook

Alistair McCallum

OXFORD
UNIVERSITY PRESS

Welcome

1 **Write the answers.**

1 seven + six = <u>*thirteen*</u>

2 nineteen – eight = _____

3 four + twelve = _____

4 twenty ÷ two = _____

5 five x three = _____

6 eighteen – one = _____

2 **Circle the ten colors (➔ or ↓) in the wordsearch. Then write the words.**

N	R	E	D	U	W	L	A	P
W	A	S	B	R	O	W	N	U
H	P	G	L	I	L	Y	E	R
I	O	R	A	N	G	E	L	P
T	F	E	C	H	E	L	X	L
E	N	E	K	A	B	L	U	E
P	I	N	K	R	O	O	B	Y
A	C	B	Y	O	I	W	E	S

1 <u>*black*</u>

2 _____

3 _____

4 _____

6 _____

6 _____

7 _____

8 _____

9 _____

10 _____

3 **Do the crossword.**

Down   **Across**

1 r		2		3				
u								
l								
4 e								
r								
		5						
	6							

4 Write the days and months in the correct order.

Days of the week
1 _____Monday_____
2 _____
3 _____
4 _____
5 _____
6 _____
7 _____

Saturday

July

October

Monday

February

Thursday

September

Wednesday

March

Sunday

May

December

June

Tuesday

Friday

August

April

November

January

Months of the year
1 _____January_____
2 _____
3 _____
4 _____
5 _____
6 _____
7 _____
8 _____
9 _____
10 _____
11 _____
12 _____

5 Complete the puzzle.

22 | t | w | e | n | t | y | – | t | w | o |
81 ... – ...
50 ...
46 ... – ...
74 ... – ...
98 ... – ...
27 ... – ...
39 ... – ...
65 ... – ...

What's this number? Write it here: [   ]

6 Fill in the blanks with the words below.

| what | mean | can | how | you |

1 _____How_____ do you spell 'London'?
2 What does 'desk' _____?
3 _____ you repeat that, please?
4 How do _____ say 'bonita' in English?
5 _____ page is it?

Unit 1

Vocabulary

1 Look at the map. Fill in the blanks with the countries below.

> the United States   Japan   Russia   the United Kingdom

1   Hi! I'm from _____*the United States*_____ .   2   Hello! I'm from _____ .

3   He's from _____ .   4   Hello! We're from _____ .

2 Circle the words (→ or ↓ or ↘) in the wordsearch. Then fill in the blanks with the correct country.

Extend your vocabulary

A	R	V	O	F	L	A
F	I	N	S	R	A	N
C	H	I	N	A	T	G
O	P	G	E	N	B	E
D	R	E	M	C	E	T
C	A	R	R	E	P	N
A	L	I	X	U	T	O
O	C	A	N	A	D	A

Peru
China
Nigeria
France
Canada

1   ____*Peru*____ is in South America.
2   _____ is in Europe.
3   _____ is in Asia.
4   _____ is in North America.
5   _____ is in Africa.

4

Grammar

1 Look at the pictures. Fill in the speech bubbles with the phrases below.

> We're from France.   He's from Nigeria.   I'm fourteen.
> John is my friend.   She's thirteen.   They're from China.

THE INTERNATIONAL SCHOOL

John is my friend.

1 David and John, 13, U.K.

2 Lee and Lin, 15, China

3 Jose, 14, Peru

4 Adewole, 13, Nigeria

5 Michel, 14, and Monique, 15, France

6 Amy, 13, Canada

2 Circle the correct words.

1 Jose **are** / **is** fourteen. **He's** / **We're** from Peru.

2 Lee **is** / **am** from China. **He** / **She** is fifteen.

3 'Hi! **I'm** / **We're** Lin. Lee **are** / **is** my friend.'

4 John and David **are** / **is** from the United Kingdom. **He's** / **They're** thirteen.

5 'Hello! I'm Michel. **I'm** / **We're** fourteen. Monique **are** / **is** my friend.
   He's / **She's** fifteen. **They're** / **We're** from France.'

3 These sentences are wrong. Write the correct sentences. Use short forms.

1 Amy is from Peru. _No! She's from Canada_ .

2 Lee and Lin are thirteen. _____.

3 Adewole is from Japan. _____.

4 Monique is sixteen. _____.

5 David and John are from France. _____.

Vocabulary

1 Fill in the blanks with the nationality.

1 I'm from Los Angeles in the United States. I'm _____*American*_____.

2 We're from Barcelona in Spain. We're _____.

3 I'm from Edinburgh in the United Kingdom. I'm _____.

4 He's from Saint Petersburg in Russia. He's _____.

5 We're from Tokyo in Japan. We're _____.

6 I'm from Melbourne in Australia. I'm _____.

7 My friends are from Cape Town in South Africa. They're _____.

8 I'm from Recife in Brazil. I'm _____.

9 We're from San José in Guatemala. We're _____.

10 She's from Guadalajara in Mexico. She's _____.

2 What nationality are they? Unscramble the words and fill in the blanks.

Jose, Peru

Lee and Lin, China

Adewole, Nigeria

1 He's ___*Peruvian*___. arePuvin

2 They're _____. eshiCne

3 He's _____. egiriNan

Michel and Monique, France

Amy, Canada

4 They're _____. crehFn

5 She's _____. idaCnana

Extend your vocabulary

Grammar

1 **Put the words in order to make questions.**
Then match the questions with the answers.

1   your What's name? _What's your name_____?   A I'm from France.
2   you old How are? _____?   B I'm thirteen.
3   from Where you are? _____?   C My name's Celia.

2 **Fill in the blanks with the words below.**

> I'm   What's   from   Where
> name's   are   How

Jon: Hi! What's your name?
Carl: My (1) __name's__ Carl.
Jon: (2) _____ are you from?
Carl: I'm (3) _____ Australia.
Jon: (4) _____ old (5)_____ you?
Carl: (6) _____ sixteen.

Carl   Jon

3 **You are Rachel. Fill in the blanks.**

Rachel: Hello! What's (1) _your name_?
Mitsuo: My name's Mitsuo.
Rachel: Where (2) _____ _____ _____?
Mitsuo: I'm from Tokyo in Japan. I'm Japanese.
Rachel: How (3) _____ _____ _____?
Mitsuo: I'm sixteen.

Mitsuo, 16, Tokyo, Japan

4 **Write the questions and complete the answers.**

Mitsuo: (1) _What's your name_?
Rachel: My (2) _name's_ Rachel.
Mitsuo: (3)_____ _____ _____ _____?
Rachel: I'm (4) _____ _____ in the United Kingdom.
               I'm (5) _____.
Mitsuo: (6)_____ _____ _____ _____?
Rachel: (7) _____ _____.

Rachel, 15, London, U.K.

Unit 2

Vocabulary

1 Unscramble the jobs and complete the puzzle.

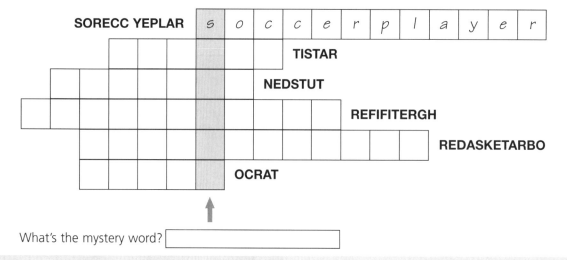

SORECC YEPLAR | s o c c e r p l a y e r

TISTAR

NEDSTUT

REFIFITERGH

REDASKETARBO

OCRAT

What's the mystery word?

2 Match the people with the words below.

builder | 3 | police officers | | guitarist | | reporter | | taxi driver |

Extend your vocabulary

Grammar

Name	Richard	Marcos	Hazel	Chen	Fayola	Cathy
Nationality	British	Brazilian	British	Chinese	Nigerian	Australian
Age	32	44	30	18	18	22
Job	Actor	Doctor	Doctor	Student	Model	Police officer

1 **Look at the chart. Put the words in order to make sentences.**

1 Hazel / not / French / is <u>Hazel is not French</u> .

2 not / policeman / a / Richard / is _____ .

3 'Russia / I / from / not / am' _____ . (Chen)

4 eighteen / not / is / Marcos _____ .

5 'are / students / We / not' _____ . (Richard and Cathy)

6 models / not / Marcos and Hazel / are _____ .

2 **Complete the sentences with *isn't* or *aren't*.**

1 Marcos <u>isn't</u> a student.

2 Cathy _____ from the United Kingdom.

3 Richard and Fayola _____ doctors.

4 'We _____ sixteen. We're eighteen!' (Fayola and Chen)

5 Hazel _____ twenty. She's thirty.

6 'We _____ singers. We're doctors!' (Marcos and Hazel)

7 You _____ a teacher. You're a student!

3 **These sentences are wrong. Write the correct sentences. Use short forms.**

1 Cathy is a doctor.
   <u>She isn't a doctor</u>. <u>She's a police officer</u>.

2 Chen is Russian.
   He _____. _____.

3 Marcos and Hazel are actors.
   They _____. _____.

4 Fayola is sixteen.
   She _____. _____.

5 Richard and Hazel are from France.
   They _____. _____.

Vocabulary

1 Do the crossword.

Down

							¹h
							a
²	³		⁴				p
							p
			⁵				y
	⁶						

Across

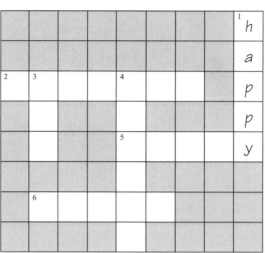

2 Fill in the blanks with the words below.

| wet | sick | excited | sleepy | busy |

I'm _wet_.

1

We're _____.

2

I'm _____.

3

I'm _____.

4

We're _____.

5

Extend your vocabulary

Grammar

Luis

Carmen

Vincent

1 **Look at the pictures. Match the people with the sentences.**

1 (I'm hot!)   a   Kate and Linda

2 (I'm happy!)   b   Vincent

3 (We're cold!)   c   Luis

4 (I'm wet!)   d   Fiona

5 (We're excited!)   e   Eric and Peter

6 (I'm sick!)   f   Carmen

Kate and Linda

2 **Circle the correct words.**

1 Fiona **is** / (**isn't**) happy. (**She's**)/ **She** sick.
2 Luis **is** / **are** happy.
3 Kate and Linda **isn't** / **aren't** sad. They're **excited** / **exciteds**.
4 Eric and Peter **are** / **is** cold.
5 Vincent isn't hot. **She's** / **He's** wet.

Fiona

3 **These sentences are wrong. Write the correct sentences. Use short forms.**

1 Kate is sick.
   She isn't sick . _She's excited_ .

2 Eric and Peter are hot.
   _____ . _____ .

3 Luis is sad.
   _____ . _____ .

4 Carmen is cold.
   _____ . _____ .

Eric and Peter

Unit 3

Vocabulary

1 Write the opposites of the adjectives.

1 old _____new_____   2 long _____   3 cheap _____   4 big _____

2 Label the pictures with the correct adjective.

 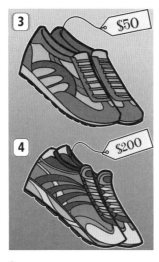  

1 _____short_____   3 _____   5 _____   7 _____
2 _____   4 _____   6 _____   8 _____

3 Fill in the blanks with the words below.

| thin | clean | heavy | dirty | light | thick |

1 His bag is ___heavy___.   2 Her bag is _____.   3 Her book is _____.

4 His book is _____.   5 The dog is _____.   6 The dog is _____.

Grammar

1 **Look at the pictures. Fill in the blanks with the words below.**

our	his	their	my	her

Angelo   Mai   Susan   Colin

1 ___His___ computer is new.   2 _____ CD player is expensive.   3 _____ bags are heavy.

4 _____ cell phones are small.

5 _____ dog is dirty!

Eva   Tony   Spot   Sergio

2 **Circle the correct possessive adjective.**

1 Angelo's friend: 'He's from Mexico. **Her** / **His** name is Angelo. He's **my** / **your** friend.
    His / **Their** computer is new. It's fantastic!'

2 Tony and Eva's friend: 'Tony and Eva are **my** / **their** friends. **Her** / **Their** cell phones
    are small. They're excellent!'

3 Sergio's friend: 'Hi, Sergio. Wow! **Your** / **Our** dog is very dirty!'

3 **Write affirmative and negative sentences about the people in the picture.**

1 Angelo / computer / old Angelo's _computer isn't old_____ . His _computer is new_____ .
2 Mai / CD player / cheap Mai's _____ . Her _____ .
3 Susan and Colin / bags / light _____ . _____ .
4 Sergio / dog / clean _____ . _____ .

Vocabulary

1 **Look at Danny's family tree. Fill in the blanks with the correct word.**

1 Mike and Rita are Danny's __parents__ .

2 Robert is Danny's _____.

3 Jane is Danny's _____.

4 Martha and Kate are Danny's
   _____.

5 Mike is Danny's _____.

6 Andrew is Danny's _____.

7 Andrew and Jane are
   Danny's_____.

8 Rita is Danny's _____.

Andrew   +   Jane

Mike   +   Rita

Robert   Danny   Martha   Kate

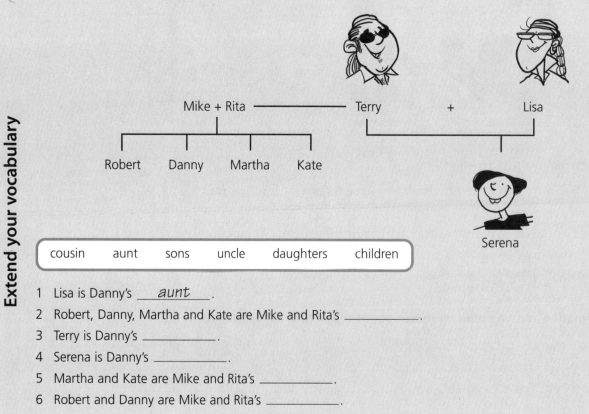

2 **These are some more people in Danny's family. Fill in the blanks with the words below.**

Mike + Rita ——————— Terry   +   Lisa

Robert   Danny   Martha   Kate

Serena

Extend your vocabulary

| cousin | aunt | sons | uncle | daughters | children |

1 Lisa is Danny's __aunt__ .

2 Robert, Danny, Martha and Kate are Mike and Rita's _____.

3 Terry is Danny's _____.

4 Serena is Danny's _____.

5 Martha and Kate are Mike and Rita's _____.

6 Robert and Danny are Mike and Rita's _____.

Grammar

1 Look at the photos. Fill in the blanks with *is*, *isn't*, *are* or *aren't*.

Nico: (1) __Is__ she your sister?
Danny: No, she (2) _____. She's my cousin!
Nico: (3) _____ he your father?
Danny: No, he (4) _____. He's my uncle!
Nico: (5) _____ he a musician?
Danny: Yes, he (6) _____.
         He's a guitarist. He's cool!

Nico: (7) _____ they your parents?
Danny: No, they (8) _____. They're my
         grandparents!
Nico: (9) _____ they from the United
         Kingdom?
Danny: Yes, they (10) _____. They're
         from London.

2 Write questions and answers about the photo.

(1) ___Are they___ Danny's cousins?
No, (2) ___they aren't___. They're his sisters.
(3) _____ students?
Yes, (4) _____.

(5) _____ Danny's father?
Yes, (6) _____. He's a police officer.
(7) _____ Danny's mother?
Yes, (8) _____.
(9) _____ a police officer?
No, (10) _____. She's a teacher!

3 Answer the questions.

1 Are you a teacher? __No, I'm not__. __I'm a student__.
2 Are you from the United Kingdom? _____. _____.
3 Are you thirty years old? _____. _____.

Unit 4

Vocabulary

1 Unscramble the words.

1 trosef _forest_   2 elka _____   3 omuninat _____   4 verri _____   5 hecab _____

2 Fill in the blanks with the singular or plural of the words.

1 Are they penguins?
No! They are _dolphins_.

2 Is it a whale?
No! It's a _____.

3 Are they seals?
No! They are _____.

4 Is it a dolphin?
No! It's a _____.

3 Look at the picture. Fill in the blanks with the plurals of the words below.

Extend your vocabulary

| chicken | dog | cow | goat | cat |

1 There are two _cats_.   3 There are two _____.   5 There are five _____.
2 There are three _____.   4 There are four _____.

Grammar

1 Look at the postcard. Fill in the blanks with *There is*, *there is*, *There are*, or *there are*.

Hi David!

POSTCARD

Yellowstone National Park is awesome! <u>There</u> <u>are</u> big mountains, and _____ _____ a beautiful lake. I'm in the forest right now. _____ _____ bears in the forest! There aren't any beaches, but _____ _____ a long river.
Bye!

Maria

2 Look at Maria's photos from her vacation. Complete the conversation.

David: (1) <u>Is</u> <u>there</u> a forest in the park?

Maria: Yes, (2) _____ _____. And (3) _____ _____ goats in the mountains.

David: (4) _____ _____ any cats and dogs?

Maria: No, (5) _____ _____.

David: (6) _____ _____ any beaches?

Maria: No, (7) _____ _____.

David: (8) _____ _____ a river?

Maria: Yes, (9) _____ _____. The river is cold!

Vocabulary

1 Where are they? Fill in the blanks with the correct words.

Hi Dad! I'm in the _music store_!

Hi Emma! I'm in the _____ - _____!

Hi Toni! I'm in front of the _____ _____!

Hi Dad! I'm in the _____ _____!

Hi Peter! I'm in the _____ _____!

Hi Carmen! I'm in the _____ _____!

2 Match the photos with the words below.

library [3]   police station [ ]   school [ ]   fire station [ ]   hospital [ ]

Extend your vocabulary

Grammar

1 **Look at the map. Fill in the blanks with the words below.**

> between   next to   in front of   across from

1 The bus stop is __between__ the police station and the restrooms.
2 The girl is _____ the police station.
3 The cyber café is _____ the movie theater.
4 The restrooms are _____ the library.

2 **Write questions and answers about the map.**

1 __Where's__ the taxi?
  It's __in front of__ the movie theater.
2 _____ the students?
  They're _____ the library.
3 _____ the police station?
  It's _____ the cyber café.
4 _____ the fire station?
  _____ the police station.
5 _____ the movie theater?
  _____ the library and the cyber café.

Unit 5

Vocabulary

1 Circle (→ or ↓ or ↘) the eight objects in the wordsearch. Then write the words.

T	Y	C	A	M	E	R	A	T	O	L	C
N	E	A	N	P	R	A	S	B	A	E	D
T	E	L	E	V	I	S	I	O	N	O	P
O	M	C	E	E	P	L	K	B	I	A	L
R	I	U	F	P	U	E	T	N	T	Y	A
Z	U	L	T	A	H	R	C	A	Q	R	Y
G	G	A	M	E	C	O	N	S	O	L	E
R	E	T	P	S	I	J	N	Z	D	A	R
B	W	O	F	I	N	X	O	E	E	D	E
R	A	R	A	D	I	O	U	S	N	A	N
S	T	E	R	E	O	M	Q	I	O	J	P

1 _camera_
2 _____
3 _____
4 _____
5 _____
6 _____
7 _____
8 _____

2 Label the pictures with the words below.

| mouse | printer | monitor | mousepad | keyboard |

2 [_____]

3 [_____]

1 [monitor]

4 [_____]

5 [_____]

Extend your vocabulary

Grammar

1 Write sentences with *This, That, These or Those*.

1 <u>This is my</u> sister.

2 _____ brothers.

3 _____ parents.

4 _____ dog!

2 Write questions and answers.

What's this?

1 <u>This is a calculator</u> .

_____ ?

2 _____ .

_____ ?

3 _____ .

_____ ?

4 _____ .

Vocabulary

1 Write the names of the objects below.

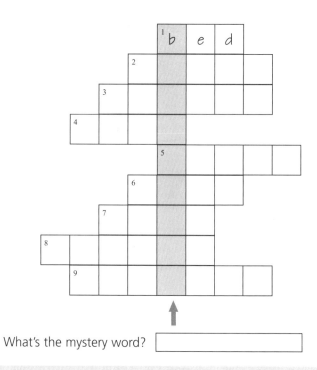

What's the mystery word? [   ]

2 Look at the picture of the kitchen. Write the number next to the words below.

refrigerator [2]   stove [ ]   washing machine [ ]   clock [ ]   plates [ ]   sink [ ]

Extend your vocabulary

Grammar

1 Look at the pictures. Write the plurals.

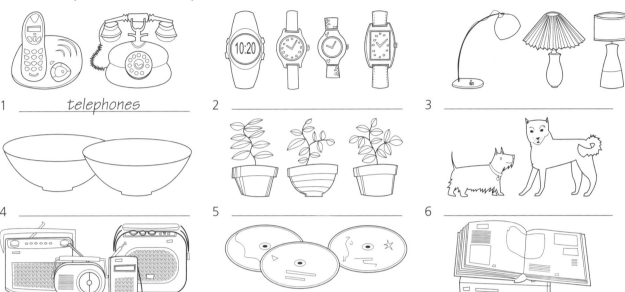

1 ___telephones___

2 _____

3 _____

4 _____

5 _____

6 _____

7 _____

8 _____

9 _____

2 Write sentences about these pictures. Use *on, in or under* and the plural form.

1 cup / desk

There are ___three cups on___ the desk.

2 box / bed

_____.

3 CD / bed

_____.

4 dog / box

There are _____ the box.

5 glass / desk

_____.

6 book / bookcase

_____.

Unit 6

Vocabulary

1 Find eight activities in the word snake. Then write the words.

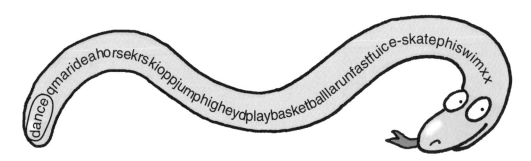

1 _____dance_____   3 _____   5 _____

2 _____   4 _____   6 _____

2 Look at the pictures. Label the pictures with the words below.

> drive   sing   draw   play the guitar   cook   speak French

1 _____sing_____

2 _____

3 _____

4 _____

5 _____

6 _____

Extend your vocabulary

Grammar

1 **Match 1–5 with A–E.**

1 An actor
2 A mechanic
3 A guitarist
4 A dancer
5 A soccer player

A can dance.
B can play soccer.
C can act.
D can play the guitar.
E can fix cars.

2 **Look at the chart. Fill in the blanks with *can* or *can't*.**

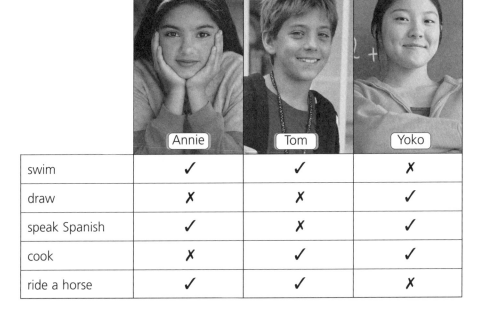

	Annie	Tom	Yoko
swim	✓	✓	✗
draw	✗	✗	✓
speak Spanish	✓	✗	✓
cook	✗	✓	✓
ride a horse	✓	✓	✗

1 Tom _can_ cook.
2 Yoko _____ ride a horse.
3 Tom and Annie _____ swim.

4 Annie _____ draw.
5 Annie _____ cook.
6 Annie and Yoko _____ speak Spanish.

3 **Write questions and answers about Annie, Tom and Yoko.**

Yoko

1 _Can_ _she_ draw?   Yes, _she_ _can_ .
2 _____ _____ swim?   No, _____ _____ .

Annie and Tom

3 _____ they ride a horse?   Yes, _____ _____ .
4 _____ _____ draw?   _____ , _____ _____ .

Tom

5 _____ _____ speak Spanish?   _____ _____ _____ .
6 _____ _____ cook?   _____ _____ _____ .

Vocabulary

1 Circle the words (→ or ↓ or ↘) in the wordsearch. Then write the words.

C	R	K	I	C	K	E
T	O	U	C	H	C	S
A	H	I	T	N	W	I
P	O	R	W	L	A	C
L	A	T	O	R	L	N
E	B	S	R	W	K	S
N	I	O	S	A	R	L
F	A	H	L	E	T	O

1 p*ass*_____
2 h_____
3 w_____
4 k_____
5 t_____
6 t_____

2 Match the pictures with the instructions below.

Catch the ball! 4 Stand up! ☐ Don't fall over! ☐ Dive into the water! ☐ Don't drop the ball! ☐

Extend your vocabulary

26

Grammar

1 **Circle the correct instruction for the place.**

1 Ice-skating rink: Fall over! / (Don't fall over!)

2 Classroom: Listen to the teacher! / Don't listen to the teacher!

3 Baseball game: Drop the ball! / Don't drop the ball!

4 English lesson: Speak English! / Don't speak English!

5 Tennis game: Hit the ball! / Don't hit the ball!

2 **Put the words in order to make sentences.**

1 the / classroom / don't / in / run

   Don't run in the classroom _____ !

2 brother / don't / your / hit

_____ !

3 drive / fast / don't

_____ !

4 touch / glass / don't / the

_____ !

5 in / don't / lake / swim / the

_____ !

Unit 7

Vocabulary

1 Complete the verbs.

1 g _e_ _t_ _u_ p   7:00 AM

2 _ o t_ _ _ h _ _l   (clock)

3 _ _ v _ _ _ n _ _   (clock)

4 f _ _ _ _ _ _ _l _ _ _ _ _   (clock)

5 _ a _ _ _ _ e _ _ _ _ _ _   7:15 AM

6 _ _ t _ _ _ _ _   (clock)

7 _ _ m _ _ _ m _ _ _ _ _   5:00 PM

8 _ _ _ r _ _ _ s _ _ _   (clock)

9 _ _ _ e _ i _ _ _ _   (clock)

10 _ _ _ o _ _ _ d   10:00 PM

2 Label the pictures with the words below.

| visit my grandparents | buy a sandwich | listen to music | take a shower | take the bus |

1 _take a shower_

2 _____

3 _____

4 _____

5 _____

Extend your vocabulary

Grammar

1 **Circle the correct word.**

1 I watch TV **at** / **in** the evening.

2 We **go** / **have** breakfast at seven thirty in the morning.

3 I take the bus to school **at** / **in** eight o'clock in the morning.

4 I **am** / **go** to bed at eleven o'clock.

5 I **have** / **do** a shower in the morning.

6 We **get** / **do** our homework after school.

2 **Write sentences about the pictures. Use the simple present.**

1 We _____*have lunch at twelve thirty*_____ .

2 I _____ .

3 They go _____ .

4 We _____ classes _____ .

5 I _____ .

6 I _____ in the evening.

Vocabulary

1 Circle (↔ or ↕ or ↘) the eight verbs in the wordsearch. Then write the words.

L	K	R	O	W	Y	T	O	F	U	T	R
I	S	F	Z	R	D	A	K	H	Z	N	S
V	B	L	H	X	R	S	O	O	R	I	R
E	M	T	A	M	D	E	I	O	A	A	Z
Y	R	L	S	U	R	F	A	X	S	P	Z
D	E	Z	G	Z	M	K	Y	D	I	L	S
R	P	U	U	M	C	E	J	B	Z	B	J
N	N	A	A	T	U	D	J	H	F	J
I	J	F	U	B	Q	E	G	J	L	N	C
X	P	F	V	L	D	M	E	O	V	L	N
O	Z	T	M	L	K	R	V	M	G	L	U
Q	F	K	K	M	W	E	B	W	V	U	P

1 l_ive_____
2 w_____
3 s_____
4 r_____
5 m_____
6 p_____
7 l_____
8 r_____

2 Fill in the blanks with the correct words.   _____

> shop   garage   office   bank   factory   supermarket

1 She works in a ___garage___.

2 He works in a _____.

3 She works in a _____.

4 They work in a _____.

5 They work in a _____.

6 He works in an _____.

Extend your vocabulary

Grammar

breakfast:	7:00	Mom	7:00	Dad
go to work:	walk to school 8:00		bus to hospital 7:30	
work:	9:00 – 4:30 (lunch 1:00)		8:30 – 5:00 (lunch 12:30)	
after work:	music		book	
dinner:	8:00		8:00	
evening:	friends		TV	
bed:	11:00		11:00	
weekend:	beach	Debbie, teacher	beach	Max, doctor

1 **Look at the chart about Jerry's mom and dad. Circle the correct word.**

1 Debbie and Max are Jerry's parents. They (live) / **lives** in Chicago.

2 They **have** / **has** breakfast at seven o'clock.

3 Max **work** / **works** in a hospital.

4 Debbie **walk** / **walks** to school at eight o'clock.

5 Max **start** / **starts** work at eight thirty in the morning.

He **finish** / **finishes** work at five o'clock in the afternoon.

6 Debbie **have** / **has** lunch at one o'clock.

7 They **go** / **goes** to bed at eleven o'clock.

2 **Fill in the blanks in these sentences about Max and Debbie.**

Max

1 He _takes_ _the_ _bus_ to work at seven thirty.

2 He _____ _____ at twelve thirty.

3 After work, he _____ a book.

4 He _____ TV _____ _____ evening.

Debbie

5 She _____ work at nine o'clock. She _____ work at four thirty in the afternoon.

6 After work, she _____ _____ music.

7 She _____ her _____ in the evening.

Max and Debbie

8 They _____ _____ at eight o'clock in the evening.

9 They _____ _____ _____ at eleven o'clock.

10 On the weekend, they _____ _____ _____ _____ .

Unit 8

Vocabulary

1 Match the sentences with the pictures.

A

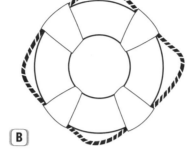

B

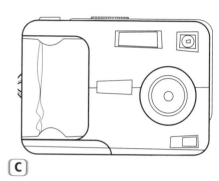

C

1 She sings. _E_
2 He takes photos. __
3 He climbs mountains. __
4 She rescues people. __
5 He interviews people. __

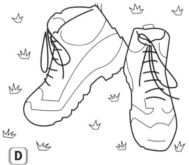

D

E

2 Fill in the blanks with the words below.

Extend your vocabulary

| travel around the world | fly a helicopter | write articles | fix cars |

1 I'm a pilot. I ___fly a___ ___helicopter___ .

2 I'm an explorer. I ___ _____ .

3 I'm a mechanic. I ___ _____ .

4 I'm a journalist. I ___ _____ for magazines.

Grammar

	Miguel, Mexico	Jane, U.K.	Alex, U.K.
live	Acapulco	London	Manchester
get up	7:00	7:00	7:30
go to school	walk	bus	walk
lunch	12:30, home	12:30, school	1:00, school
evening	movies	guitar	TV
weekend	beach	friends	soccer

1 **Look at the chart. Circle the correct verb form.**

1 Jane (**comes**) / **doesn't come** from the United States.

2 Miguel **goes** / **doesn't go** to the beach in the evening.

3 Alex **plays** / **doesn't play** soccer on the weekend.

4 Jane **takes** / **doesn't take** the bus to school.

5 Alex **has** / **doesn't have** lunch at home.

6 Miguel **lives** / **doesn't live** in Veracruz.

7 Jane and Miguel **get up** / **don't get up** at 7:00.

2 **Fill in the blanks with *don't* or *doesn't*.**

1 Miguel ___*doesn't*___ watch TV in the evening.

2 Alex and Jane _____ have lunch at home.

3 Jane _____ get up at 6:00.

4 Alex _____ live in London.

5 Miguel and Alex _____ take the bus to school.

3 **These sentences are wrong. Write the correct sentences.**

1 Jane lives in Manchester.
 _She doesn't live in Manchester___. _She lives in London_____.

2 Alex takes the bus to school.
He _____. _____ to school.

3 Miguel and Jane get up at eight o'clock.
They _____. _____ seven o'clock.

4 Jane plays the piano in the evening.
_____ in the evening. _____ the guitar.

5 Miguel goes to the movies in the morning.
_____ morning . _____ evening.

6 Alex and Jane come from France.
_____. _____ the UK.

Vocabulary

1 Match each picture with three words.

long   wavy   dark   curly   straight   short   dark   blond   long

1 _____long_____   4 _____   7 _____

2 _____   5 _____   8 _____

3 _____   6 _____   9 _____

2 Find eight words in the word snake. Then label the picture with the words.

cheekteeth hair nosechineyemouthear

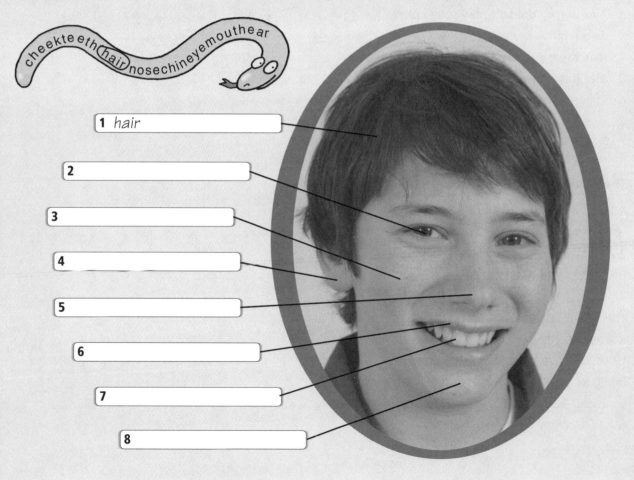

1 _hair_

2 _____

3 _____

4 _____

5 _____

6 _____

7 _____

8 _____

Grammar

Mandy
age: *17*
eyes: *brown*
hair: *straight, blond*
height: *short*

Dan
age: *17*
eyes: *blue*
hair: *wavy, blond*
height: *short*

Mark
age: *70*
eyes: *blue*
hair: *curly, gray*
height: *tall*

Mizuki
age: *30*
eyes: *brown*
hair: *short, black*
height: *tall*

1 **Match the descriptions with the names.**

1 I'm tall. I don't have blue eyes. I have short hair.

2 I'm seventeen. I have blond hair. I don't have brown eyes.

3 I'm tall. I have blue eyes. I don't have black hair.

4 I'm seventeen. I have brown eyes. I don't have curly hair.

a Mark
b Mandy
c Dan
d Mizuki

2 **Circle the correct words in these sentences.**

1 Mizuki **is** / **has** thirty. She **is** / **has** black hair.

2 'I **am** / **are** tall. I **have** / **has** blue eyes.'

3 Mandy and Dan **don't have** / **doesn't have** dark hair.

4 Mark **have** / **has** blue eyes. He **don't have** / **doesn't have** brown eyes.

5 Mizuki and Mandy **don't have** / **doesn't have** blue eyes. They **have** / **has** brown eyes.

3 **Write sentences about the people in the pictures. Write one negative sentence and one affirmative sentence.**

1 Mark / seventeen / seventy.
   Mark isn't seventeen. _He's seventy_.

2 Mizuki / blond hair / black hair.
   Mizuki doesn't _____. She _____.

3 Dan / green eyes / blue eyes.
   _____. _____.

4 Mark and Mizuki / short / tall
   _____. They _____.

5 Mandy and Dan / dark hair / blond hair.
   _____. _____.

Unit 9

Vocabulary

1 Circle (→ or ↓) the eight places in the wordsearch. Then write the words.

E	A	C	D	T	E	K	I	D	O	V	U
N	C	O	U	N	T	R	Y	L	U	N	V
F	I	N	L	A	H	E	M	T	O	D	S
C	B	C	N	B	E	A	C	H	O	A	W
A	Z	E	O	R	M	H	W	B	S	N	L
N	I	R	J	D	E	T	O	W	E	C	A
F	E	T	C	I	P	A	R	T	Y	E	N
U	R	A	V	T	A	J	P	E	O	C	I
S	O	C	C	E	R	G	A	M	E	L	E
M	B	E	W	Q	K	Y	W	N	L	U	T
I	S	P	O	R	T	S	C	L	U	B	R
T	L	N	E	X	O	T	E	S	R	D	S

1 <u>sports</u> <u>club</u>
2 t_____ p_____
3 d_____ c_____
4 s_____ g_____
5 p_____
6 b_____
7 c_____
8 c_____

2 Fill in the blanks with the words below.

café   shopping mall   movies   restaurant   theater   zoo

1 On the weekend, he goes to the <u>movies</u>.

2 He goes to the _____.

3 They go to a _____.

4 They go to a _____.

5 We don't go to the _____.

6 We go to the _____.

Extend your vocabulary

Grammar

Anna

every day	school
evening	music
Saturday	friends, tennis
Sunday	beach

Anna's parents, Carlos and Monica

every day	work
evening	TV
Saturday	soccer games (dad)
	shopping mall (mom)
Sunday	country

1 **Complete this conversation between Anna and her friend Tim.**
Fill in the blanks with *do, don't, does* or *doesn't*.

Tim: (1) __*Do*__ you go to school?

Anna: Yes, I (2) _____. I go to school every day.

Tim: (3) _____ you watch TV in the evening?

Anna: No, I (4) _____. I listen to music in the evening.

Tim: (5) _____ your parents go to work?

Anna: Yes, they (6) _____. They go to work every day.

Tim: (7) _____ your dad go to soccer games?

Anna: Yes, he (8) _____. He goes to soccer games on Saturday.

Tim: (9) _____ your mom go to soccer games?

Anna: No, she (10) _____.

2 **Answer the questions about Anna and her parents.**

1 Does Ann go to school every day? _Yes_, __*she does*__.

2 Does Anna go to the country on the weekend? _____, _____.

3 Do Anna's parents watch TV in the evening? _____, _____.

4 Does Anna's dad go to work? _____, _____.

5 Do Anna's parents play tennis? _____, _____.

Vocabulary

1 Make five adjectives and five movie types with the letters below.

1 VELO TOSRY   _LOVE_   _STORY_

2 BIRNOG   _____

3 TARMICNO   _____

4 NCTIAO VIOME   _____ _____

5 CYDOME   _____

6 XITNEIGC   _____

7 ROHROR IMVEO   _____ _____

8 FYNNU   _____

9 RYASC   _____

10 SEINECC COTFNII OMEIV   _____ _____ _____

2 Match the TV programs with the pictures.

music show **2**   game show ⬜   cartoon ⬜   nature documentary ⬜

1

2

3

4

Extend your vocabulary

Grammar

	Melissa	Greg	Mr. Watson
horror movies	✓	✓	✗
rock music	✓	✓	✓
game shows	✗	✓	✗
tennis	✓	✗	✓
computer games	✗	✓	✗
parties	✓	✓	✗
basketball	✗	✗	✓

1 Look at the chart. Put the words in order to make sentences.

1 doesn't / horror movies / like / Mr. Watson _Mr. Watson doesn't like horror movies_ .

2 game shows / likes / Greg _____ .

3 like / Melissa and Mr. Watson / computer games / don't _____ .

4 parties / Greg and Melissa / like _____ .

5 Melissa / doesn't / game shows / like _____ .

2 Answer the questions about Greg, Melissa and Mr. Watson.

1 Does Greg like computer games?
   Yes, he does .

2 Does Mr. Watson like parties?
   _____ .

3 Do Melissa and Greg like horror movies?
   _____ .

4 Does Melissa like tennis? _____ .

5 Do Greg and Melissa like basketball?
   _____ .

3 Write questions and answers.

1 you / nature documentaries ☺
   Do you like nature documentaries? _Yes, I do_ .

2 we / music shows ☹
   _____ ? _____ .

3 he / concerts ☺
   _____ ? _____ .

4 they / theme parks ☺
   _____ ? _____ .

5 she / cartoons ☹
   _____ ? _____ .

6 you / soccer ☹
   _____ ? _____ .

Unit 10

Vocabulary

1 What do people do at parties? Complete the puzzle.

1 ___give___ presents

2 _____ a cake

3 wear nice _____

4 _____ the room

5 _____ CDs

6 _____ cards

7 _____ a concert

g	i	v	e			

Fill in the blanks with the shaded words. At the party, we _____ _____ !

2 Match the pictures with the words below.

clean the room [3] buy food [ ] send invitations [ ] move the furniture [ ] wash the dishes [ ]

Extend your vocabulary

Grammar

1 Write questions and answers. Use the words in the chart.

When	do you like game shows?	They go to the beach.
Where	do you get up?	She takes the bus.
What	do your parents do on the weekend?	At seven o'clock in the morning.
How	does your mom go to work?	He lives in Boston.
Why	does your uncle live?	Because they're funny!

1 *When do you get up*   ? *At seven o'clock in the morning*   .
2 _____? _____.
3 _____? _____.
4 _____? _____.
5 _____? _____.

2 Circle the correct question word.

Veronica: Hi, Daniel. (1) (**Where**) / **When** do you live?

Daniel: I live on Fourth Avenue.

Veronica: (2) **What** / **When** do you start classes?

Daniel: I start classes at eight thirty.

Veronica: (3) **What** / **Where** do you do after school?

Daniel: I do my homework. In the evening, I visit Ron.

Veronica: (4) **When** / **Where** does Ron live?

Daniel: He lives on North Street.

Veronica: (5) **How** / **Why** do you visit Ron?

Daniel: Because he's my best friend!

3 Write the questions for Veronica.

Veronica: (1) Hi, Sonja. *Where do you* go on Saturday?

Sonja: I go to the sports club.

Veronica: (2) _____ to the sports club?
Do you walk?

Sonja: No, I don't. I take the bus.

Veronica: (3) _____ do at the sports club?

Sonja: I play tennis with my friends.

Veronica: (4) _____ home?

Sonja: I go home at twelve thirty.

Veronica: (5) _____ lunch?

Sonja: I have lunch at home with my family.

Vocabulary

1 **Unscramble the letters and fill in the blanks.**

1 My brother ____watches____ TV every day. (sehwcat)

2 I go out with _____ twice a week. (drifsne)

3 My sister _____ books every evening. (daser)

4 I never play computer _____. (megsa)

5 They go to the _____ once a month. (yarbril)

6 We play a _____ sport twice a week. (amet)

7 She goes _____ once a week. (mimwgins)

8 I talk on the _____ every day. (henop)

9 My dad _____ the net three times a week. (fruss)

10 My parents go _____ once a week. (igphospn)

2 **Label the pictures with the words below.**

| go to the dentist   take exams   go on vacation   practice the piano   visit my cousin |

1 ____visit my cousin____   2 _____   3 _____

4 _____   5 _____

Extend your vocabulary

Grammar

	Leo	Claudia, Leo's sister	Juan, Leo's brother
swimming	every day	never	every Saturday
movies	twice a week	every Sunday	never
computer games	never	every day	three times a week
dentist	twice a year	twice a year	once a year
TV	three times a week	four times a week	every day
exams	once a year	three times a year	once a year

1 **Look at the chart about Leo and his brother and sister. Circle the correct words in the sentences.**

1 How often **do** / **(does)** Claudia play computer games?

She **play** / **plays** computer games every day.

2 How often **do** / **does** Juan go to the movies?

He never **go** / **goes** to the movies.

3 How often **do** / **does** Leo and Juan take exams?

They **take** / **takes** exams once a year.

2 **Complete the conversation between Leo and his friend Ricky.**

Ricky: How often (1) ___*do*___ ___*you*___ ___*watch*___ TV?

Leo: I watch TV three times a week.

Ricky: How often (2) _____ _____ _____ to the dentist?

Leo: I go to the dentist twice a year.

Ricky: How often (3) _____ your sister (4) _____ swimming?

Leo: She (5) _____ _____ swimming.

Ricky: How often (6) _____ your brother (7) _____ TV?

Leo: (8) _____ _____ TV (9) _____ _____ .

3 **Write questions and answers.**

1 Claudia / movies

How often does Claudia go to the

movies ?

She goes to the movies once a week .

2 Leo / computer games

_____?

_____.

3 Leo and Claudia / dentist

_____?

_____.

4 Juan / swimming

_____?

_____.

Unit 11

Vocabulary

1 Label the pictures with the correct verb.

1 _____pull_____

2 _____

3 _____

4 _____

5 _____

6 _____

7 _____

8 _____

2 Find six words in the word snake. Then label the pictures with the words.

drinksleepsmilecookdrawthink

Extend your vocabulary

1 _____smile_____

2 _____

3 _____

4 _____

5 _____

6 _____

Grammar

1 Write the *-ing* form of the verbs.

1 have _having_
2 run _____
3 smile _____
4 play _____
5 write _____
6 sit _____

2 Write the sentences with *I, you, he, she, it, we* or *they*. Use short forms.

1 The boy is shouting. _He's shouting_ .
2 I am dancing. _____ .
3 You are listening to music. _____ .
4 The girls are laughing. _____ .
5 The girl is taking a photo. _____ .
6 The boys are running. _____ .
7 The dog is sleeping. _____ .
8 My friend and I are surfing the Net.
_____ .

3 Write about the picture with the verbs below. Use short forms.

do	sleep	talk	read	laugh	draw

1 _____She's talking_____ on the phone.
2 _____ a book.
3 _____ .
4 _____ .
5 _____ a picture.
6 _____ his homework.

Vocabulary

1 Match the sentences with the rooms in the house.

1 He's cooking.
2 We're relaxing.
3 They're having lunch.
4 She's sleeping.
5 They're playing.
6 I'm taking a shower.

a yard
b dining room
c bathroom
d kitchen
e bedroom
f living room

2 Fill in the blanks with the words below.

| floor   shelf   rug   wall   ceiling |

Extend your vocabulary

1 She's putting books on the ___*shelf*___.
2 He's painting the _____.
3 She's putting a picture on the _____.
4 It's sleeping on the _____.
5 He's sitting on the _____.

Grammar

1 **Circle the correct word.**

1 My sister is **danceing** / (**dancing**).

2 My dad **isn't** / **aren't** working today.

3 It's seven o'clock. My mom is **geting** / **getting** up.

4 I'm not **listening** / **listen** to music. **I** / **I'm** watching TV.

5 They **isn't** / **aren't** having dinner right now.

6 We're **taking** / **takeing** photos of the concert.

2 **Look at the picture. Write negative and affirmative sentences.**

1 The students / have lunch / have a class
   The students aren't having lunch. *They're having a class*.

2 They / study Spanish / study English
   They aren't _____. They're _____.

3 Mr. Jones / write on the wall / write on the board
   Mr. Jones isn't _____. _____.

4 Olivia / sit next to the teacher / sit next to Marco
   _____. _____.

5 Marco / talk to his friend / listen to the teacher
   _____. _____.

Unit 12

Vocabulary

1 Circle (→ or ↓) the six *-ing* forms in the wordsearch. Then fill in the blanks with the correct words.

T	A	M	W	A	P	L	I	D	C	O	L
K	F	I	M	S	I	V	S	H	G	N	A
R	E	N	B	H	R	E	T	Z	L	C	M
E	X	C	H	A	N	G	I	N	G	A	N
C	S	U	E	K	S	T	U	W	P	R	E
Q	T	L	G	I	N	W	A	K	I	R	S
W	A	V	I	N	G	B	C	E	K	Y	L
A	W	P	C	G	O	M	I	O	U	I	K
C	N	R	A	E	X	T	S	L	E	N	G
J	O	F	O	L	L	O	W	I	N	G	C
E	G	L	N	V	M	A	K	I	N	G	I

1 The man and the woman are _exchanging_ briefcases.

2 Look at that dog! Is it _____ us?

3 My dad is _____ hands with the teacher.

4 Where's mom? Is she _____ a cake?

5 Look at those people! Are they _____ at us?

6 She's _____ a heavy suitcase.

2 Look at the picture. Match the pictures with the words below.

wait for [2]   talk to [ ]   look for [ ]   listen to [ ]   look at [ ]

Bubbles! Where are you?

Extend your vocabulary

48

Grammar

1 **Fill in the blanks with** *am, 'm not, is, isn't, are,* **or** *aren't.*

1   _Are_ you listening to a CD?

Yes, I _____.

2   _____ your sister doing her homework?

No, she _____. She's talking on the phone!

3   _____ your parents having a party?

No, they _____. They're having dinner.

4   _____ the dog playing in the yard?

Yes, it _____.

5   _____ you going to bed now?

No, I _____. I'm going out!

2 **Put the words in order to make questions.**

1   making / you / a phone call / are?

Are you making a phone call ?

2   he / Is / a newspaper / reading?

_____?

3   Are / shaking / they / hands?

_____?

4   waving / Is / at us / she?

_____?

3 **Write questions and answers about the people in the picture.**

1   go / to the bank / to the library

_____Is she going_____ to the bank?

No, _she isn't_. _She's going_ to the library.

2   sit / in the classroom / in the café

_____?

_____.

3   talk / to a doctor / to a police officer

_____?

_____.

4   eat / a pizza / a burger

_____?

_____.

5   wait / for a bus / for a taxi

_____?

_____.

Vocabulary

1 Do the crossword.

Down

1 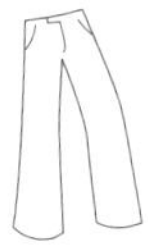

2 

3 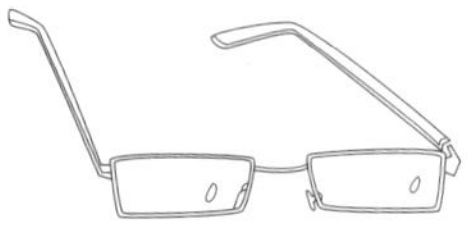

4 

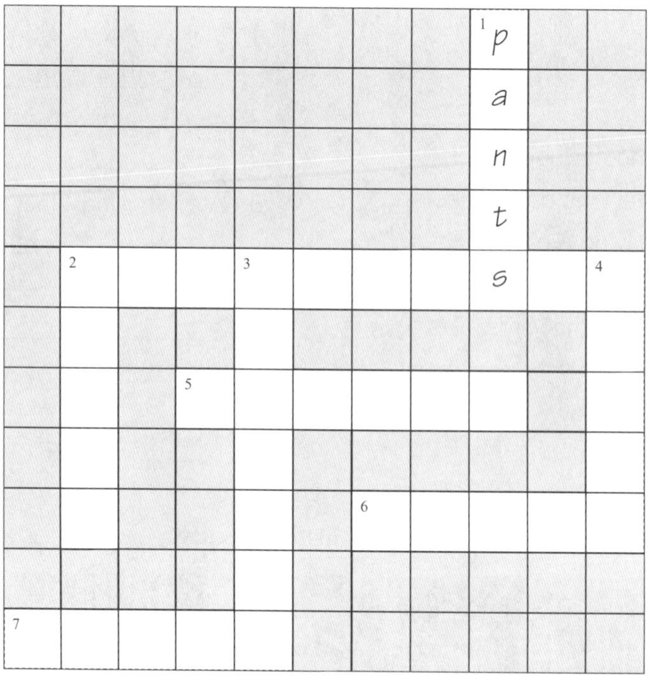

Across

2 

5 

6 

7 

Extend your vocabulary

2 Fill in the blanks with the words below.

gloves   sneakers   T-shirt   cap   shorts   socks

1 *T-shirt*

2 ______

3 ______

4 ______

5 ______

6 ______

Grammar

1 **Match the questions with the answers.**

1 What is he wearing?
2 Where are they going?
3 Why are you laughing?
4 What is she doing?
5 Why are they shouting?
6 What is he making?

a Because this program is funny.
b A pizza.
c Blue pants and a white T-shirt.
d Because they're angry.
e To New York.
f She's riding a bike.

2 **Circle the correct word.**

1 (**What**)/ **Why** is she carrying? She's carrying a suitcase.
2 Where **is** / **are** we going? We're going home!
3 Why **is she** / **she is** running? Because she's late!
4 **Where** / **What** are they doing? They're walking to school.
5 Where is he **sit** / **sitting**? Next to the window.

3 **Complete Tom's questions.**

Tom: Hi, Maria! (1) _____*What*_____ are you doing?

Maria: Hi, Tom! I'm at home with my brother Jose and my parents. I'm watching TV.

Tom: What (2) _____ watching?

Maria: I'm watching Secret Agent. It's exciting!

Tom: (3) _____ Jose doing?

Maria: He's decorating the room.

Tom: (4) _____ decorating the room?

Maria: Because there's a party tomorrow. It's his birthday! Mom's in the kitchen.

Tom:.   (5) _____ making?

Maria: She's making a cake for the party. Dad isn't helping. He's sleeping.

Tom: (6) _____ sleeping?

Maria: (7) On the sofa!

Extra reading 1

OXFORD BOOKWORM STARTERS

Girl on a Motorcycle

Early the next morning, Kenny puts on the TV in his room. A news-reader is talking about the supermarket robbery. There are some pictures from the supermarket camera.

Kenny watches the news.
'The robber is somebody with long blond hair, and with a motorcycle,' says the newscaster.
Suddenly, Kenny remembers the girl at the motel desk. 'Is it her?' he thinks. 'Is she the robber?'

He goes for breakfast. The girl is eating her breakfast at a table near the window. Kenny looks at her. 'Is it her?' he thinks. 'I think I know her, but . . .' He walks across to her table.
'Can I sit here?' he asks.
The girl looks up. 'Well . . . OK,' she says.

1 Circle the correct answer.

1 Kenny is **at home** / **in a motel** / **in the hospital**.

2 The newscaster is talking about a robbery at a **supermarket** / **motel** / **bank**.

3 The robber has **brown** / **blond** / **black** hair.

4 The robber has a **car** / **bicycle** / **motorcycle**.

2 When Kenny sees the girl at the café, what does he think? Check (✔) one answer.

1 'She's the robber.' ☐

2 'She isn't the robber.' ☐

3 'Is she the robber? I don't know.' ☐

3 What do you think? Check (✔) *Yes* or *No* for each sentence.

	Yes	No
1 The girl is the supermarket robber.	☐	☐
2 She has a gun.	☐	☐
3 Kenny calls the police.	☐	☐

Extra reading 2

Taxi of Terror

1 **Match the people in the taxi with the descriptions.**

1 the taxi driver   a   is in the boot of the taxi.

2 the Wolf   b   is driving the taxi.

3 Jack   c   is the man with the gun.

2 **Circle T (True) or F (False).**

1 Jack calls the police. (T) / F

2 Jack can see a big clock. T / F

3 The Wolf has a gun. T / F

3 **What happens at the end of the story? Check (✔) *Yes* or *No* for each sentence.**

	Yes	No
1 The Wolf shoots the taxi driver.	☐	☐
2 The police find the taxi.	☐	☐
3 The Wolf goes to prison.	☐	☐

Glossary

boot (British English) = trunk (American English)

Extra reading 3

Starman

A big red car drives on a long, long road. In the car is a farmer, Bill. He is hot and tired. He wants to go home and have a bath.

Bill listens to the radio in his car and he sings. Bill likes singing. Sometimes people like Bill's singing – but not very often.

The song he is singing is called Hot, hot, hot.

There is a sign on the side of the road. Bill reads it: Goondiwindi, 72 kilometers. Dirranbandi 136 kilometers. Bill must drive for a long time. His home is about a hundred kilometers away.

He rubs his eyes. The sun is very hot and the road is long. Bill does not want to go to sleep so he sings some more. A kangaroo hears him and jumps away. Bill laughs, then rubs his eyes again.

Just then Bill sees something. Suddenly he is not tired and he is not laughing. The hair on his head stands up. There is something on the road.

He stops the car and gets out. The thing is a long way in front of Bill. He cannot see what it is – but he does not like it.

Bill gets back in his car and drives slowly. The thing is moving – it is alive.

'What the . . .' Bill says quietly. 'It's a man! What's a man doing here?'

---

1 Circle the correct word.

1 Bill is a (farmer) / doctor.

2 The weather is very **hot** / **cold**.

3 The road is very **busy** / **quiet**.

2 Fill in the blanks with the words below.

> sitting   tired   home   scared   sees

Bill is going (1) _home_ .

He is (2) _____ .

Suddenly he (3) _____ a man.

The man is (4) _____ in the road.

Bill is (5) _____ .

3 What do you think about the man? Where is he from? Check (✔) *Yes* or *No* for each sentence.

		Yes	No
1	The man is sick.	☐	☐
2	The man is from space.	☐	☐
3	The man is dangerous.	☐	☐

Extra reading 4

OXFORD BOOKWORM STARTERS

Give us the money

1 **Circle T (True) or F (False).**

1 For Adam, every day is different. T / (F)

2 Adam is an actor. T / F

3 Serena is an actor. T / F

2 **Fill in the blanks with the words below.**

> money   making   thieves   stealing   actors

The people in the park are (1) _actors_ .

They are (2) _____ a film.

The men in the bank are (3) _____ .

They are (4) _____ a lot of (5) _____ .

3 **Now Adam has the money. What happens at the end of the story? Check (✔) one sentence.**

1 Adam keeps the money. ☐

2 The thieves get the money. ☐

3 Adam gives the money back to the bank. ☐